SUCCESS
COMES FROM
SERVICE

THE "5 F" FRAMEWORK

MAKE WINNING A HABIT

JUSTIN LAFITTE

MERACK

Published and distributed by Merack Publishing.

Lafitte, Justin
Success Comes From Service: The "5 F" Framework, Make Winning A Habit

ISBN 978-1-957048-77-2

To Glenna, my compass. I love you.

IF YOU ARE NOT ACTIVELY SEEKING TO MEET THE 5 Fs, THIS BOOK IS NOT FOR YOU!

faith: you have an unwavering faith in Christ as your Savior.

family: you believe that your relationships with family and friends are the currency of life. you are intentional and engaging.

fitness: you take care of yourself physically, both with your nutrition and your exercise.

foster: you are, or are doing the things to become, a top 10%er in your work/craft, metrics, results, consistency, etc... you are doing the things necessary to be in the top 10% of your industry (i.e. you foster your craft/work to achieve the most).

finances: you steward your wealth, short and long term. you invest and don't spend frivolously. you educate yourself and make wise decisions with your money.

CRITICAL QUESTION:

If someone who does *not* know you were to thoroughly observe you for a day, would they recognize the 5 Fs in you?

If the answer to that question is "yes," let's proceed...

PREFACE

There are no secrets in this book! None. What is in this book, though, will change your life. How? Through systematic and focused discipline, rooted in accountability and trust. This sounds rigid, and it is... but it will absolutely set you free and allow you to enjoy and live life at a level that you didn't think was possible.

In the process of writing this book, I adopted all of the techniques you are about to implement, just to help prove this process and how it guides you to hitting your goals. Stated another way, I practiced the exact process that is preached in this book, simply to write the book!

The examples and stories I will reference are real experiences that were learned not only through trial and error myself, but with many clients as well. The amount of time spent researching and developing this content is extensive because I wanted to make sure that once this book was released, it could get someone from simply dreaming about something to actually accomplishing that thing through a guided process.

I am honored to be able to release this process to you and can't wait to hear about your success!

INTRO

Success comes from service. It's a relatively self- explanatory statement, but let's dive in a bit more to make sure we're on the same page here:

I believe achieving anything noteworthy in life is directly dependent on how well you provide service. Usually that is service to others, but it also applies to yourself.

At a high level, look at massive companies like Amazon, Apple, Nike, etc. They all provide a lot of people with products that those customers value. So the connection is: quality product + demand + volume = high success for those companies. Now on a smaller scale in a totally different scenario, let's look at a marriage: a successful marriage consists of two people who intentionally find ways to serve each other. If they don't do that, the marriage will likely fail. It's not rocket science. A successful, massive company and a successful marriage have the same key ingredients: there is value provided, creating the desire for this outcome on a repeated basis, and then both parties reciprocate this for each other, thus success.

- If you want a successful relationship with God, serve Him through prayer and evangelizing.

- If you want a successful relationship with your significant other, serve them through proactive intentionality and patience.

- If you want a successful eating and fitness routine, serve yourself by being diligent and aware.

- If you want a successful business, focus on serving your customers.

- If you want to create lasting wealth, serve your investments via diligence and research.

It all connects; serving yourself and others will lead to success. It always has and always will.

DAY ZERO

On the next page, you will be establishing a goal from each of the 5 Fs of your life:

FAITH
FAMILY/FRIENDS
FITNESS
FOSTER
FINANCES

Here's a couple real-life examples:

EXAMPLE ONE:

- 10 minutes of prayer, upon waking up
- 1 hour per day, no phone, just family
- 45 minutes of exercise, before 7am
- 10 outbound calls per day to prospects
- 15 minutes of investment research

EXAMPLE TWO:

- 15 minutes of devotions before 6am
- 1 intentional call/text to family/friend
- palm-size portions for all meals
- 1 hour of new client research
- 30 minutes investment podcasts

There is a science behind accomplishing a task, immediately checking it off, and then moving forward. You have to stack up small, daily wins in order to trigger the level of goal setting/hitting that we will be working on throughout this book and your life.

Get it done, check it off, repeat it, create habits, establish the lifestyle, and move mountains through your results.

They say it takes 21 days to create a habit... so we will do 28 days just to be thorough.

After you've established your goals with the next page, take the rest of today to focus and meditate on them.

Now it's your turn. Identify an achievable but challenging goal from each of the 5 F's of your life:

FAITH:

_____

FAMILY/FRIENDS:

_____

FITNESS:

_____

FOSTER

_____

FINANCES

_____

If you are reading this digitally, write down your goals in a notebook
that you can keep handy, or type out your goals in a note on your phone.

(If you're having trouble determining your goals,

email me at justin@scfsgroup.com and I will help you out!)

Now that you have established your list for the next 7 days, it's time to go through and write it down for tomorrow. Check these off as you go. Meaning: keep the book/checklist with you wherever you go.

IMPORTANT: You should only write down each day's goals the morning of, or the night before.

Remember to take the rest of today to focus and meditate on your goals and be mentally, emotionally, and physically prepared to start this journey tomorrow morning. Plan, prepare, and persevere!

SEE YOU TOMORROW.

WEEK
ONE

DAY ONE

"There's no progress made in the comfort zone."

UNKNOWN

FAITH:

_____

_____

FAMILY/FRIENDS:

_____

_____

FITNESS:

_____

_____

FOSTER:

_____

_____

FINANCES:

_____

_____

Notes and Thoughts:

YOUR INITIALS FOR WINNING THE DAY: _____

DAY TWO

"If nothing changes, then nothing changes."

COURTNEY C. STEVENS

FAITH:

_____

_____

FAMILY/FRIENDS:

_____

_____

FITNESS:

_____

_____

FOSTER:

_____

_____

FINANCES:

_____

_____

Notes and Thoughts:

YOUR INITIALS FOR WINNING THE DAY: _____

DAY THREE

"Your input determines your outlook."

ZIG ZIGLAR

FAITH:

_____

_____

FAMILY/FRIENDS:

_____

_____

FITNESS:

_____

_____

FOSTER:

_____

_____

FINANCES:

_____

_____

Notes and Thoughts:

YOUR INITIALS FOR WINNING THE DAY: _____

DAY FOUR

"Spend time with people that fit your future, not your past."

UNKNOWN

FAITH:

_____

_____

FAMILY/FRIENDS:

_____

_____

FITNESS:

_____

_____

FOSTER:

_____

_____

FINANCES:

_____

_____

Notes and Thoughts:

YOUR INITIALS FOR WINNING THE DAY: _____

14

DAY FIVE

"Don't be a discount version of yourself."

UNKNOWN

FAITH:

_____

_____

FAMILY/FRIENDS:

_____

_____

FITNESS:

_____

_____

FOSTER:

_____

_____

FINANCES:

_____

_____

Notes and Thoughts:

YOUR INITIALS FOR WINNING THE DAY: _____

DAY SIX

"Pay attention to who you're with when you feel your best."

UNKNOWN

FAITH:

_____

_____

FAMILY/FRIENDS:

_____

_____

FITNESS:

_____

_____

FOSTER:

_____

_____

FINANCES:

_____

_____

Notes and Thoughts:

YOUR INITIALS FOR WINNING THE DAY: _____

DAY SEVEN

"Powerful presence comes from being powerfully present."

UNKNOWN

FAITH:

_____
_____

FAMILY/FRIENDS:

_____
_____

FITNESS:

_____
_____

FOSTER:

_____
_____

FINANCES:

_____
_____

Notes and Thoughts:

YOUR INITIALS FOR WINNING THE DAY: _____

SCFS TIMEOUT:

"The dedicated time to my personal interest (side project) was something that I hadn't previously been making time for. I had wanted to do it, but I allowed myself to neglect my desire to make progress. As soon as I committed dedicated time daily towards the pursuit of it, I experienced rapid growth and development. This was exciting and fulfilling because it turned a source of frustration and discontentment previously (my neglect of this personal interest) into a source of fulfillment and enjoyment."

———

"One thing that I've been struggling with my whole life is becoming a morning person and starting my day earlier. I am a person who wants to do so much in a 24 hour window and the only way to do that is by starting my day at 5:30 AM. SCFS has helped me cultivate a new habit of starting my day at this time every day. I used to be a person who dreaded the mornings and couldn't get out of bed for anything. Now I go to bed looking forward to starting my day at 5:30, getting my morning meditation in and crushing my workout. This new routine and practice in my life has given me more energy throughout the rest of my day and clarity as to when certain things will be getting done. I used to sporadically go to the gym depending on the events of the day. Now I have a set time that it gets done every single day and that has given me a newfound peace of mind."

———

These individuals found success quickly because of their attention to detail on the objectives in their life that were important to them. They've always cared, but their intentional focus was the difference maker!

WEEK ONE WRAP-UP

Congratulations on completing your first week! If you've been pushing yourself, you are already noticing changes. You should be feeling more energized at the beginning and end of the day, being more mindful of what you're eating, having more intentional conversations with family and friends, and just being more aware of what you're doing and why! This is NOT a phase... this is you! This is the path you are supposed to be on and it's leading you to the best version of you. One day at a time, you are transforming what you are capable of and bringing an incredible amount of value to yourself and those around you.

What measurable progress have you noticed within the 5 Fs in this first week?

Faith:_____

Family/Friends:_____

Fitness:_____

Foster:_____

Finances:_____

What is your overall assessment of yourself in Week One?

What tweaks do you need to make to your daily objectives? What accomplishments will you see 7 days from now?

One week is now written in the new book of your life... What's the next chapter going to look like?

WEEK
TWO

DAY EIGHT

"People follow someone who is always real;
not someone who is always right."

UNKNOWN

FAITH:

_____

_____

FAMILY/FRIENDS:

_____

_____

FITNESS:

_____

_____

FOSTER:

_____

_____

FINANCES:

_____

_____

Notes and Thoughts:

YOUR INITIALS FOR WINNING THE DAY: _____

DAY NINE

"Don't just be a sponge that soaks it up. You have to go scrub!"

JUSTIN LAFITTE

FAITH:

_____
_____

FAMILY/FRIENDS:

_____
_____

FITNESS:

_____
_____

FOSTER:

_____
_____

FINANCES:

_____
_____

Notes and Thoughts:

YOUR INITIALS FOR WINNING THE DAY: _____

DAY TEN

"Our greatest glory is not in never falling,
but in rising every time we fall."

CONFUCIUS

FAITH:

_____

_____

FAMILY/FRIENDS:

_____

_____

FITNESS:

_____

_____

FOSTER:

_____

_____

FINANCES:

_____

_____

Notes and Thoughts:

YOUR INITIALS FOR WINNING THE DAY: _____

DAY ELEVEN

"When you focus on making sure those around you have a great day, you'll have no choice but to have a great day yourself."

UNKNOWN

FAITH:
_____
_____

FAMILY/FRIENDS:
_____
_____

FITNESS:
_____
_____

FOSTER:
_____
_____

FINANCES:
_____
_____

Notes and Thoughts:

YOUR INITIALS FOR WINNING THE DAY: _____

DAY TWELVE

"What you say isn't your identity. Your habits are your identity."
JAMES CLEAR

FAITH:

_____

_____

FAMILY/FRIENDS:

_____

_____

FITNESS:

_____

_____

FOSTER:

_____

_____

FINANCES:

_____

_____

Notes and Thoughts:

YOUR INITIALS FOR WINNING THE DAY: _____

DAY THIRTEEN

"You don't lose. You only win or learn."

NELSON MANDELA

FAITH:

_____
_____

FAMILY/FRIENDS:

_____
_____

FITNESS:

_____
_____

FOSTER:

_____
_____

FINANCES:

_____
_____

Notes and Thoughts:

YOUR INITIALS FOR WINNING THE DAY: _____

DAY FOURTEEN

"The fear of judgment leads to being a liar. Be vulnerable."

UNKNOWN

FAITH:

_____

_____

FAMILY/FRIENDS:

_____

_____

FITNESS:

_____

_____

FOSTER:

_____

_____

FINANCES:

_____

_____

Notes and Thoughts:

YOUR INITIALS FOR WINNING THE DAY: _____

SCFS TIMEOUT:

Most people like their goals in life; but they are not desperate for them.

They like the idea of their goals

Most aren't willing to do the things they actually have to in order to get to their goals.

The most alive you will ever feel is when you are desperate and have a grand desire to achieve something.

Be desperate for your goals, and you will focus on them in a way you never have before.

Your "calling" just means you have a destiny to work hard at something.

It does not mean it's easy.

There's a mythology about greatness nowadays...

People think it just happens.

They don't see the hard work put in by the people who do make it.

It can sometimes take months or years to see the results (good and bad) of what you're doing today.

Don't let your ego get in the way of understanding that there is delayed gratification from your efforts!

WEEK TWO WRAP-UP

Two weeks in... Objectives should now start to feel like habits. Your body and mind should start to feel like they are on auto-pilot with the decisions you're making. Intentionality is your standard! If it doesn't feel this way, you need to assess if your daily objectives are truly aligning with your goals!

Now let's review…

What measurable progress have you noticed within your 5 Fs of life in the second week?

Faith:_____

Family/Friends:_____

Fitness:_____

Foster:_____

Finances:_____

What is your overall assessment of yourself in Week Two?

What adjustments will push you on your daily objectives?

What results are you determined to see next week?

Two weeks! The "Book of (your name)" is a great read... I look forward to reading the next chapter in a week!

WEEK
THREE

DAY FIFTEEN

"Think like a millionaire. Hustle like you're broke."

UNKNOWN

FAITH:

_____

_____

FAMILY/FRIENDS:

_____

_____

FITNESS:

_____

_____

FOSTER:

_____

_____

FINANCES:

_____

_____

Notes and Thoughts:

YOUR INITIALS FOR WINNING THE DAY: _____

DAY SIXTEEN

"A goal without a deadline is just a dream."

NAPOLEON HILL

FAITH:

_____

_____

FAMILY/FRIENDS:

_____

_____

FITNESS:

_____

_____

FOSTER:

_____

_____

FINANCES:

_____

_____

Notes and Thoughts:

YOUR INITIALS FOR WINNING THE DAY: _____

DAY SEVENTEEN

"Be the best you. Everyone else is taken."

OSCAR WILDE

FAITH:

_____

_____

FAMILY/FRIENDS:

_____

_____

FITNESS:

_____

_____

FOSTER:

_____

_____

FINANCES:

_____

_____

Notes and Thoughts:

YOUR INITIALS FOR WINNING THE DAY: _____

DAY EIGHTEEN

*"Write something worth reading,
or do something worth writing about."*

BENJAMIN FRANKLIN

FAITH:

_____

_____

FAMILY/FRIENDS:

_____

_____

FITNESS:

_____

_____

FOSTER:

_____

_____

FINANCES:

_____

_____

Notes and Thoughts:

YOUR INITIALS FOR WINNING THE DAY: _____

DAY NINETEEN

"Do today what others won't so you can
do tomorrow what others can't."

JERRY RICE

FAITH:

_____

_____

FAMILY/FRIENDS:

_____

_____

FITNESS:

_____

_____

FOSTER:

_____

_____

FINANCES:

_____

_____

Notes and Thoughts:

YOUR INITIALS FOR WINNING THE DAY: _____

DAY TWENTY

"You can't go back and change the beginning.
You can start where you are and change the ending."

C.S. LEWIS

FAITH:

_____

_____

FAMILY/FRIENDS:

_____

_____

FITNESS:

_____

_____

FOSTER:

_____

_____

FINANCES:

_____

_____

Notes and Thoughts:

YOUR INITIALS FOR WINNING THE DAY: _____

40

DAY TWENTY-ONE

"Humility isn't thinking less of yourself. It's thinking of yourself less."

C.S. LEWIS

FAITH:

_____

_____

FAMILY/FRIENDS:

_____

_____

FITNESS:

_____

_____

FOSTER:

_____

_____

FINANCES:

_____

_____

Notes and Thoughts:

YOUR INITIALS FOR WINNING THE DAY: _____

SCFS TIMEOUT:

In the mind, there is no difference between what is real and what is imagined. You can literally think about anything you want to. **Anything**. No one can stop you from thinking about whatever you want to right now.

Go ahead; give it a shot and think about something outlandish... A once-in-a-lifetime trip. A mansion. Climbing a mountain. Hanging with your favorite celebrity. Seriously though, take some time and think about a massive aspiration of yours.

(30 sec. pause to think about your biggest aspiration!)

Maybe someone else has accomplished this before. Maybe no one ever has. Here's the deal: eventually your thoughts will become your new reality if you follow this path...

Thoughts > Motivation > Behaviors > Actions > Habits > Results > Reality

It **must** happen in that order though! Simple concept. Difficult journey. Anybody who has accomplished any historical feat in this world followed this path. They all started with a simple thought, the same thoughts you and I have access to. They didn't stop at thinking though. They took the next step.

The people who do take action find a way to step forward with their thoughts. The people who **don't** take action abandon their thoughts in their mind. Your thoughts are absolutely contagious. They're what drive you to what is next. (Warning: The same rule applies for negative thoughts! Thoughts can be dangerous!)

You share at least one thing in common with the greatest athletes, entrepreneurs, inventors and influencers in the world.

We have all been blessed with the same opportunity to **think about anything we want to**.

So, here's the parting challenge:

What are your biggest aspirations?

What are you going to do next to turn those into a reality?

Thoughts > Motivation > Behaviors > Actions > Habits > Results > Reality

WEEK THREE WRAP-UP

They say it takes 21 days to create a habit. If your daily objectives are starting to become habits, that is great news! What it also means, though, is that it's time to tweak your daily checkpoints as we head into the final week of this workbook. No progress is made in the comfort zone!

Faith:_____

Family/Friends:_____

Fitness:_____

Foster:_____

Finances:_____

What is the best habit you've created in the last 21 days? What tweak can you make to really push you next week?

What are you most excited to be able to state about yourself in 7 days?

Prove to yourself what you're capable of this final week!

WEEK
FOUR

DAY TWENTY-TWO

"Your test becomes your testimony."
MAX LUCADO

FAITH:
_____
_____

FAMILY/FRIENDS:
_____
_____

FITNESS:
_____
_____

FOSTER:
_____
_____

FINANCES:
_____
_____

Notes and Thoughts:

YOUR INITIALS FOR WINNING THE DAY: _____

DAY TWENTY-THREE

*"People will forget what you do and say,
but not how you make them feel."*

MAYA ANGELOU

FAITH:

_____

_____

FAMILY/FRIENDS:

_____

_____

FITNESS:

_____

_____

FOSTER:

_____

_____

FINANCES:

_____

_____

Notes and Thoughts:

YOUR INITIALS FOR WINNING THE DAY: _____

DAY TWENTY-FOUR

"You can't make maximum impact doing something you tolerate."

ED MYLETT

FAITH:

_____

_____

FAMILY/FRIENDS:

_____

_____

FITNESS:

_____

_____

FOSTER:

_____

_____

FINANCES:

_____

_____

Notes and Thoughts:

YOUR INITIALS FOR WINNING THE DAY: _____

DAY TWENTY-FIVE

"Be a voice, not an echo."
ALBERT EINSTEIN

FAITH:
_____
_____

FAMILY/FRIENDS:
_____
_____

FITNESS:
_____
_____

FOSTER:
_____
_____

FINANCES:
_____
_____

Notes and Thoughts:

YOUR INITIALS FOR WINNING THE DAY: _____

DAY TWENTY-SIX

"Habits are not a line to be crossed. They are a lifestyle to live."

JAMES CLEAR

FAITH:

_____

_____

FAMILY/FRIENDS:

_____

_____

FITNESS:

_____

_____

FOSTER:

_____

_____

FINANCES:

_____

_____

Notes and Thoughts:

YOUR INITIALS FOR WINNING THE DAY: _____

DAY TWENTY-SEVEN

"Most of the time we feel tired not because we've done too much,
but because we've done too little of what makes us come alive."

JIM KWIK

FAITH:

_____

_____

FAMILY/FRIENDS:

_____

_____

FITNESS:

_____

_____

FOSTER:

_____

_____

FINANCES:

_____

_____

Notes and Thoughts:

YOUR INITIALS FOR WINNING THE DAY: _____

DAY TWENTY-EIGHT

"If it was easy, you wouldn't appreciate it."

UNKNOWN

FAITH:
_____
_____

FAMILY/FRIENDS:
_____
_____

FITNESS:
_____
_____

FOSTER:
_____
_____

FINANCES:
_____
_____

Notes and Thoughts:

YOUR INITIALS FOR WINNING THE DAY: _____

WEEK FOUR/WORKBOOK WRAP-UP:

28 straight days of commitment to your goals! That is no small accomplishment. Your impact has grown exponentially. The people around you are noticing your commitment to living at a higher level. You are noticing that certain people aren't comfortable with your changes... and that's ok! You're on a mission and your goals are built around serving others, particularly those that want to be served. Let's recap who you have become the last 28 days...

What is the single biggest change you've seen within the 5 Fs of your life in these 4 weeks?

Faith:_____

Family/Friends:_____

Fitness:_____

Foster:_____

Finances:_____

What are you most proud of overcoming?

What are you most excited to accomplish next?

If you could give a piece of advice to yourself 28 days ago, what would it be?

"Shelf" satisfaction is finding contentment in what you've accomplished and leaving it as is... That's not you though!

CALL TO ACTION:

So, now what?

Well, first of all, let me know that you have completed this book and I will send you an SCFS wristband that represents your completion of this workbook. It serves as a constant reminder of what you are doing and why.

More importantly though, finishing this book means nothing if you don't build on the progress you've made and the path that you are now on in your life.

Email me at **justin@scfsgroup.com** for the next steps on how to continue winning every single day of your life and truly living the life you were meant to live.

Whether it's a team-building opportunity, a speaking engagement for your leadership and high performers, or ongoing mentoring for yourself, there is much more for you from SCFS!

Keep up with all things SCFS on Instagram: @successcomesfromservice

**When you do things others won't do,
you will get things others won't get.**

WHAT DOES THE LADDER REPRESENT?

Ladders allow you to start at the bottom and climb to the top.

Ladders can be moved and placed where needed to in order for you to climb.

You have to take them one step at a time. You can't start at the top.

You have to climb, bottom to top, in all areas of your life.
That's why we picked a ladder.

Where will you put your ladder next?

GOAL SETTING:

As an integral part of SCFS, we want to make sure that your goals are constructed in a manner that not only challenges you, but is easy to refer to and will constantly remind you of your trajectory.

So many people go through motions; they might get a lot done, but it isn't with an end goal constantly in mind. On top of that, they don't properly adjust their goals to make sure they still align with their values and are challenging them accordingly. This leads to inefficiency, underperforming, and eventually frustration and lack of accomplishment.

With this 365-day layout, you will have short-term and long-term vision for your goals. Take your time as you work on these while also setting the bar high. You'll be amazed at what you can accomplish in a year when you win at your tasks on a daily basis.

15 minutes a day on your side project might not sound like a ton, but when you have intention behind your minutes and each day adds up, you'll find you have spent no less than 91 hours in a year on your side project. That is game-changing time right there! That's why it's so important that you set your goals accordingly. It will only happen if you schedule it.

As always, let us know if you need help. Have fun!

LOOKING
AHEAD

30 DAY GOALS:

In 30 days, what is a measurable goal you will hit for each of your 5 Fs?

Example: If you're working out 6x a week, your fitness goal could be "15 pounds lost." If your foster goal is 10 contacts a day, your goal could be "25 new sales for the month," etc.

FAITH:

_____

_____

FAMILY/FRIENDS:

_____

_____

FITNESS:

_____

_____

FOSTER:

_____

_____

FINANCES:

_____

_____

Copy this page and put it where you will see it daily as a constant reminder!
(Background on phone, car dashboard, bathroom mirror, by front door, etc.)

SEND A PICTURE TO US WHEN YOU'RE DONE.

90 DAY GOALS:

In 90 days, what is a measurable goal you will hit for each of your 5 Fs?

Keep in mind that this should be relatively aggressive and these goals may change as you discover more about yourself, but it's crucial to have these written down! Use the same format as 30-day goals: what is a measurable result you should aim for in 90 days as a result of accomplishing your daily objectives?

FAITH:

_____

_____

FAMILY/FRIENDS:

_____

_____

FITNESS:

_____

_____

FOSTER:

_____

_____

FINANCES:

_____

_____

Copy this page and put it where you will see it daily as a constant reminder!
(Background on phone, car dashboard, bathroom mirror, by front door, etc.)

SEND A PICTURE TO US WHEN YOU'RE DONE.

365 DAY GOALS:

In ONE YEAR, what is a measurable goal you will hit for each of your 5 Fs?

A year is NOT that long from now. Time flies by when you're doing life, especially when you are laser-focused on your goals. Be meticulous with writing these down, considering that these are goals that are GOING to happen. These aren't wishes; these are proclamtions! What will you be staking your claim on in a year? Be aggressive and intentional.

FAITH:

_____

_____

FAMILY/FRIENDS:

_____

_____

FITNESS:

_____

_____

FOSTER:

_____

_____

FINANCES:

_____

_____

Copy this page and put it where you will see it daily as a constant reminder!
(Background on phone, car dashboard, bathroom mirror, by front door, etc.)

SEND A PICTURE TO US WHEN YOU'RE DONE.

www.ingramcontent.com/pod-product-compliance
Lightning Source LLC
Chambersburg PA
CBHW041541120626
46551CB00019B/2785